FOREV

In 1965 a booklet entitled 'St. produced by Canon J. H. Adams M.A 1967) a renowned church historia M.C. The latter, though not a native - war and settled here in the imme

For some years the booklet has been out of print and the purpose of this reprint has been twofold - firstly, to make this delightful little history of St. Just available once again, and secondly to raise funds towards the cost of providing a new roof to the little church.

The last major works, including a new roof were carried out in 1885 and the reopening took place on June 4th of that year. The exposed situation renders the exterior and the roof especially liable to decay and damage. It is therefore remarkable that major repairs have not been needed until now. It is clear from this history that St. Just is a major part of our village's heritage, and it is imperative that the £12,000 needed for a new roof be raised. This little gem must not be allowed once again to fall into disrepair.

The reprinting of this booklet has been funded in its entirety by a few locals for whom this project has been a 'labour of love'. As a result of their generosity all monies raised by the booklet's sale will go to the 'Roof Fund' or, thereafter, the upkeep of the church itself. Particular thanks are due to Mrs. Rhoda Dearlove and Mrs. Doreen Smith for their support and donations; to Mrs. Margaret Parke for giving most generously from the sum she has raised from the sale of plants in aid of local charities; and to Mr. Don Parke for re-typing the original, adding drawings and preparation of the booklet for the publisher.

As a direct descendent of Rev. Richard Dalby, Vicar of St. Goran 1748 - 1790, who initiated the preservation of St. Just, it has given me much pleasure to make the few amendments which the passage of time has made necessary.

Archie Smith   1997

The terms' Church' and 'Chapel' have been loosely used in this account. The name 'St. Just Church' is commonly used, but in fact it is merely a Chapel of Ease to St. Goran Parish Church.

Christian worship has probably been offered in this spot for 1300 or 1400 years. The site may have been a Celtic oratory maintained and rebuilt many times by later generations, or used as a lighthouse Chapel and Chantry Chapel as well as a Chapel of Ease.

Later it was desecrated and used as a fishermen's store, although it was used simultaneously as a Nonconformist meeting house.

Now, we can worship in the beauty of holiness, so please remember that, 'The place whereon thou standest is Holy Ground.'

This *remarkable photograph was taken in August 1884, a month after the renovation of St. Just had begun. Note the absence of the roof, the eastern gable and all windows. The work was completed on June 4th. 1885.*

The Coastguard Station was completed on Oct. 15th, 1867 and the trust deeds of the Gorran Haven Congregational Church (Mount Zion) are dated Jan. 26th, 1863.

Gorran Haven, until it started to expand as a holiday resort in the late 1920's, was a very independent, closely knit, self-contained and compact community, housed in the old dwellings still existing in Church Street, Rattle Street, (lately deprived of the old cobbles) and the main road on either side of the then open stream, (but since the 1930's contained in pipes) together with Foxhole Lane and Fort.

From the earliest times fishing and farming have been the main pursuits of the inhabitants.

A writer gives the following picture derived from the Parish Registers, which gives a good idea of life in the village about 1811: - "a busy and prosperous fishing community, all of a bustle under the energetic activities of seiners, coopers, shipwrights, weavers, cordwainers, ropers and so on, to say nothing of the Preventive Service Men, who also bring their children up to the Parish Church for Baptism".

In the days before motor vehicles and the railways, Gorran Haven was very isolated with the horse drawn Carriers' Cart the only means of public transport to St. Austell. This journey was then a major event.

In those bygone days sailing coasters visited the Haven regularly. They would beach themselves and tie up under the lea of the Fort. One of the mooring rings can still be seen bedded in the rock below Colescus on the North side of the beach.

These boats brought coal from Wales and limestone from near Plymouth for burning in the Lime Kiln. Almost certainly some of the ships departed loaded with cured pilchards and pilchard oil for use for food and light in the large towns. Billingsgate Fish Market may have derived its name from the Billings of Cornwall.

There were in the Haven a number of families and clans, the chief being the Billings, Liddicoats, Pattens, Guys, Daddas and Teagues - it is regrettable that these old families are rapidly dying out.

The extent of the self sufficiency of the Haven can be gauged from the fact that the boats were made in Pill's Boatyard on the site of the present cafe and local corn was ground in the Grist Mill at one time in the main road. A house on the site bears its name.

There were several communal baking ovens, one of the last being in Zion Cottage in Church Street. In these ovens not only was bread baked, but everything else including complete dinners. Lime was of course burned in the lime kiln.

It is sad to think that these old characteristics of the seaboard are so rapidly disappearing, but it must be remembered that times were very hard and in fact right up until the end of the second world war the battle for existence was a continuous struggle.

During the early part of the century, many of the younger men used to go each summer to crew the luxury yachts which were so popular among the gentry at this time, and it was commonplace to see men wearing jerseys bearing the name of some well known yacht. Many, of course, served in the navy in one or the other of the recent wars.

Life too, was very primitive. There was no main drainage until 1935 - all was either thrown into the open stream to find its way into the sea or onto the beach down the chute on the cliff by the church. Even so Gorran Haven was quite a healthy place.

The inhabitants were stern and very religious. For many years from early Tudor times the little church was their only place of worship, and later when this became a ruin, other places including the Watch House overlooking the harbour were used.

As was to be expected in a community cut off from all large towns, their religion was rugged and austere. Largely left to themselves, they had no use for the glamour of the church and they became dissenters. The little church was used even by 'Independents' until it fell into ruins when they used the Watch House on the sea shore and later again, private houses.

THE QUAY, THE WATCH HOUSE, THE CELLARS AND THE LIME KILN

On the south side of the Haven beach lies a line of rocks called CADICROWSE - which give the beach some protection from the violent south - easterly storms often experienced in the early autumn and spring.

These rocks throughout the ages have formed the basis of the various quays built to make the harbour safer.

The present quay was built in 1885 by the Williams family of Carhayes, about the same time as the Church was re - roofed. It has recently been thoroughly repaired by public grants and subscriptions. There have been a number of earlier Quays (possibly six) all of which have been washed away by heavy seas; the original quay was built by the Bodrugans; in 1585 Peter Edgcumbe claimed ' anchorage, kalage and toll from all boats coming to the port in the Manor called Porthest or Porthust *'and to the pier there'*. Prior to the present quay there was no quay from 1820 or even earlier.

Photographs are extant showing the beach with no quay.

THE SEA FISHERY

The sea fishery at Gorran Haven is very ancient. In 1270 the Vicar is recorded as having the whole of the Altalage, i.e. all things offered on the Altar and the Small Tithe. i.e. the fishery, apples, beans and peas growing in gardens. A year later on September 22nd, 1271 this Taxatio was further amended to the effect that the Vicar should have'.....all the Altalage except from boats exceeding the number of 12 men apiece.....and the Daganae (Seines) of the Rector.' This Taxatio is of great interest, not only for its reference (one of the earliest in the country) to seine fishing, but also because the practice meant that pilchard fishing was the chief purpose of the fishery practised at Gorran Haven at that time. The importance of seine fishing continued until late in the last century when it was gradually superseded by the catching of shell fish.

ST. GORAN PARISH

The Churchtown was once called Langoran (Monastery of Goran), later corrupted to Laworan. St. Goran's first settlement was within the old Vicarage garden, part of a small estate known as Polgorran (Goran's Pool) where there is also an alleged Holy well but with no ancient remains. All of this land (i.e. Churchtown, Polgorran and Gorran Haven) formed part of the Barony of Trematon Castle and later still belonged to Phillip de Sicca Villa or Satchville. This latter granted the advowson of the Church and land to Sir Philip de Bodrugan the chief man of the parish in 1261.

In 1269 Bodrugan sold Polgorran to Bishop Bronescombe who appropriated it to his newly founded College of Glasney.

The Bodrugans of Bodrugan (Bodrugan Farm is situated on the top of the hill overlooking St. Austell Bay on the road from Port Mellon to Gorran Haven), a wild turbulent family rose to prominence in the reign of Henry 111 and continued to be the leading family in this part of Cornwall until 1487. Their fortified manor house (often erroneously called a castle) was described by Borlase as the most magnificent in Cornwall, and a great many beautiful moulded stones collected from hedges or built into walls still testify to its grandeur.

The last of the family, Sir Henry Bodrugan was really a Trenowith, his grandmother having been the heiress of Bodrugan, and his father having adopted the name. He was a stout Yorkist and after fighting for Richard the III at Bosworth, took a leading part in the Lambert Simnel rebellion against Henry V11. In doing so he lost all his possessions and only saved his life by fleeing to France. Legend has it that, hotly pursued by the King's forces led by Sir Richard Edgcumbe he rode his horse over the cliff at Chapel Point at what is now known as Bodrugan's - Leap and jumped into a boat which took him to France. Here he died in exile, having been attainted in 1487.

For his services to the King, Henry V11, Sir Richard Edgcumbe received all the Bodrugan property in St. Goran Parish, except that on the south of the Gorran Haven stream, including the quay, which passed to the Trevanyons of Carhayes, who later sold it in the early 1800's to the Williams, a noted tin mining family from Wales.

The land to the north of the stream however, though remaining in the hands of the Edgcumbes for many years was gradually sold to local farmers and others. The remnants of the estate including Bodrugan farm and several parcels of land in Gorran Haven were finally sold by auction at St. Austell in September 1918.

ST. JUST CHURCH - THE DEDICATION

Until the rediscovery of the dedication of St. Just by Charles Henderson, it had been lost for centuries, though old maps and records call the Haven Portheast, (locally pronounced Por'East). The 'u' in Cornish is pronounced 'i'. Gorran Haven is therefore a corruption of Porth Ust or Porth Just.

Who this Just was is difficult to say. In Romano - British or Celtic days the name was almost as common as John is today, and it is unlikely that he is to be identified with the patrons of either St. Just in Penwith or St. Just in Roseland. He probably came from Wales, where, as Canon Doble pointed out, a St. Just was associated with St. Gwrin at Llanwrin in Montgomeryshire, and Gwrin is probably the same as Guron or Goran.

(In Welsh the 'w' is pronounced as the 'u' is in English; Gwrin would therefore be pronounced Gurin).

THE CELTIC CHURCH

There is no evidence, documentary or otherwise, for a church on this site before the building of the present 15th century structure, though Mr. W. H. N. Cuthbert Atchley says " it is probable that parts of it rest on very ancient footings". It is surprising how many medieval chapels have disappeared leaving no trace or tradition of their existence, yet a solitary reference in some ancient document proves conclusively that they did exist. There can be very little doubt that there has been a succession of chapels on this site since Celtic days. No founder of a 15th century chapel is likely to have chosen a Celtic saint like St. Just as the patron.

The site, almost on the edge of the cliff is just such as one would expect a Celtic hermit to choose. All around the coast, on creeks or cliffs or islands are churches and chapels (or their known sites) which go back to Celtic days.

THE PRESENT CHURCH

The present church was probably erected about 1470 - 80 on the site of an earlier one by Sir Henry Bodrugan. He was knighted in 1475 and was probably the wealthiest, most powerful and most lawless landowner in Cornwall. From 1434 onwards he was continually facing charges for his outrages but was powerful enough to defy everyone till his downfall, in 1487. The chapel must have been built before this, though the architecture might suggest a slightly later date. The interior arches of the windows are precisely similar to those in the remains of the desecrated chapel at Bodrugan (only one in situ, two others have been used as fireplaces).

Besides engaging in marauding raids on his neighbours, Sir Henry occupied himself both in legitimate merchandise and unlawful piracy, and it is likely that the last two occupations rather than any devotion or care for the spiritual welfare of his tenants caused him to rebuild the ancient chapel near the cliff edge. Though originally built as oratories by Celtic Hermits many of these cliff chapels were undoubtedly used during the Middle Ages as lighthouses. At Carn Brea in St. Just in Penwith one was sited on a prehistoric tumulus and the Prior of the Mount, in a charter of 1396, confirmed to Ralph de Bolauhel " the Prebend or Chapel of St. Michael de Bree with all its tithes etc. vacant by the death of Richard Lerimiti (the hermit)....together with the money called byckenage (beaconage) receivable from the fishermen of Porthhangwin and Porthuste... " - obviously as payment for his services in keeping a light burning there to guide them home. On a rock outside Lelant a guild similarly maintained a light in a chapel there and the chapel on Rame Head served with another on the Hoe and a third on Drake's Island to provide a system of lights for the navigation of Plymouth Sound. So there is little doubt that a light in St. Just Chapel served to guide Sir Henry's ships back to the Haven just as the chapel on Chapel Point served a similar purpose for Portmellon and Mevagissey.

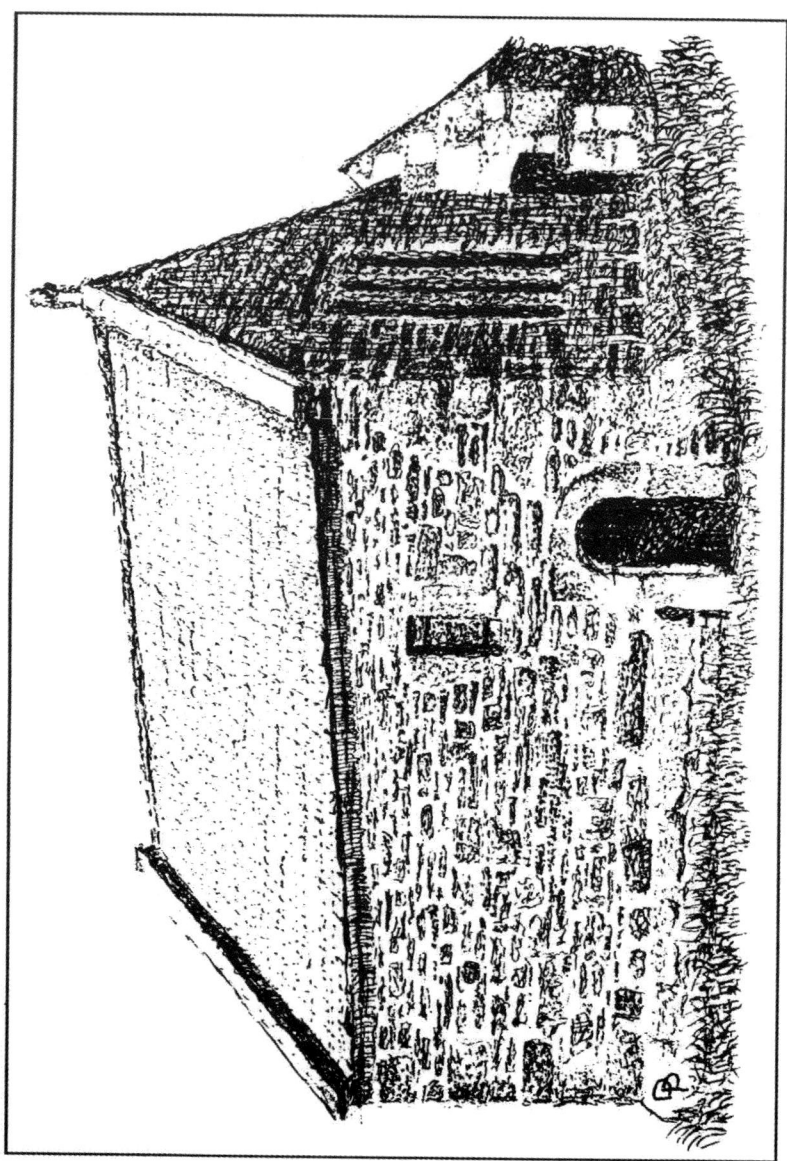

St. Clether Holy Well and Chapel. (* see page 19)

Altar and East Gable, St. Just Church, Gorran Haven. Note. This gable end is missing in the 1884 Photograph

St. Just from Rock Beach.

THE REFORMATION

Whether or not Sir Henry Bodrugan founded a chantry in St. Just must remain uncertain but it is exceedingly probable. When a landowner built or rebuilt a chapel it was natural enough for him to stipulate that one of the duties of the chaplain should be to pray for him during his life and to pray for his soul after his death, and usually for his ancestors too. Certainly Sir Henry must have realised his need for such prayers. "But not only chantries but also colleges free - chappelles, hospital, fraternities guildes and stipendarie prestes having perpetuitye for ever" were vested in the King under the Act of 1545.

Among the commissioners for Devon and Cornwall was Sir Richard Edgcumbe, and it seems hardly likely that he can have been ignorant of the existence of this chapel on his own estate even if Bodrugan was an outlying property which he seldom visited. At any rate St. Just was not included in the commissioners' returns. Like many others it was 'concealed'. The authorities were well aware of this and in the Patent Rolls of Queen Elizabeth is recorded a grant to Edw Grymstone Sr. and William le Grys, the Queen's Servant, of various lands "which premises were concealed" including in Sancte Gorani, a chapel called St. Ewste alias Juste (9 July 1569)".The Patent was to be void in respect of any of the premises which were not concealed on or before 22 July Elizabeth (1567) on or after Grymston le Grys, Wm. Drurye, the Queen's servant and others at their own costs by several commissions out of the Exchequer procured inquisitions for the discovery thereof".

It seems that Edgcumbe had already leased the chapel to local fishermen. It is even possible that he was ignorant of its existence and that it had been appropriated by them perhaps with the connivance of his steward. At any rate Grymston and le Grys seized it and sold it, but evidently it was not bought back by Edgcumbe but was probably bought by the sitting tenant or tenants.

In 1651 a former Steward of Bodrugan - in reply to queries to Piers Edgcumbe wrote as follows - "As touching the chapple when the Monasteries and Religious houses were taken off then this Chapple also fell with them and after that time the fishermen made it a house to keep their sea tackell therin ...". The bulk of the letter concerns the quay which in the 1630's was in grave disrepair "in soe much that the whole kaye was likely to fall down". The fishermen begged Sir Richard Edgcumbe to repair it and said they would relinquish all their rights in the Quay, rocks and Chapple, and, if he kept them in repair he could have the profits. Evidently they regarded the chapel as well as the quay as their property for the writer continues, "Thereupon your father did agree with certain kaye makers who came there and did amend the then break of the said kaye and repaired all other places thereof as were in decay".

Whether this phrase could be stretched to include the Chapel must be uncertain but it seems likely enough since the fishermen had mentioned the Chapel and little had been done to it for over 100 years. But if so it certainly could not be regarded as what we should call a church restoration but merely the patching up of a fishermen's store.

It remained the property of the Edgcumbes thereafter until the restoration of 1885 when the Earl transferred it to the Ecclesiastical Commissioners.

THE 17th AND 18th CENTURIES

That very little was done to St. Just Church in the mid-seventeenth century is proved by the next reference (Hals. c.1690) "In this haven town is still extant the ruins of an ancient free chapel". The description of it as a 'free' chapel can be safely ignored. Hals uses the term of nearly every chapel he mentions.

A Free Chapel was one exempt from Episcopal jurisdiction and was usually a royal foundation. But Gorran Haven is a long way from Exeter and it is likely that even if a bishop did visit the parish, Sir Henry would have steered him clear of the Haven, and that for practical purposes if not technically; he kept it as free from interference as any chapel could be.

Tonkin, who continued Hals notes from 1702-1736 speaks of a "fair Chappel with a small square tower" (actually it is pentagonal) "all stands entire but unroffed".

About 1738, William Borlase (Parochial Memoranda MS.) says merely "Remains of an ant. chappell at Goran..."

In 1745, the vicar John Dingle described it as "a chapel at Gorran Haven - a fishing town - in ruins time out of mind".

In 1763, Ecton's Thesaurus (3rd) gives under chapples "Porteast Chap. to Goran:" but Bacon's Liber Regis (a revised edition of Ecton) is obviously misinformed when it states "Porteast, chapel to Goran , demolished".

In 1779 Richard Dalby, the vicar, reported in his visitation return, "There are in Goran the remains of two chapels, neither nominated nor served in memory of man, nor does tradition say anything about them". By the curious phrase, 'nominated', Dalby probably refers to the dedication, all knowledge of which has been lost. The second chapel was presumably the one at Bodrugan. Its remains are now a farm building, divided by a floor and terribly mutilated.

The Bodrugan Chapel was first licensed in 1372 (a 14th century blocked exterior doorway remains -) but must have been enlarged by Sir Henry about the same time as he rebuilt St. Just.

Dalby continues, "As to dissenters we had three itinerant preachers for some time, but now there is one Independent in the Parish and one Independent Room over a fish cellar but no one uses it now". He gives no hint that he refers here to St. Just, but since it was undoubtedly used by Independents twenty years later it may well have been the "Independent Room over a fish cellar" referred to in 1779. If so the upper storey must have been inserted before this and some sort of roof to protect it. But we cannot be sure. If Tonkin is accurate that it was 'unroofed' in his time, then this roofing must have been after c. 1720. But he may only have judged from seeing the gable ends rising above a low flat roof invisible from below.

C. C. Gilbert (Survey of Cornwall, published 1820.), wrote "in the middle of the town stand considerable remains of an ancient chapel, and an attached tower which was also built at the expense of the Bodrugans; the roof has fallen in and the walls seem to be indebted for their preservation to the late Rev. Richard Dalby.1748 - 1790 who was at the expense of stopping up the entrance and who repaired many of the broken parts...". This must have been done between 1779 and Dalby's death in 1790, but unfortunately we cannot tell how much of the walls he may have had to rebuild.

THE 19th CENTURY

In 1812, the Congregationalists of Mevagissey started a branch in the Haven and the first service was held in an "an old Romish Chapel" on April 20th. The Congregations steadily increased to about 70 in 1851 although " the numbers in church fellowship" were then only 14.

In the vestry of the parish church is an amateur water colour painting said on an attached note to be painted about 1836 and to have come from the library at Carclew. It was probably painted by one of the family of Sir Charles Lemon. Both sides of the paper have been used. One side has a more or less finished tinted pencil sketch looking over the village (Gorran Haven) from the cliff side. The other, only roughly sketched in with a few touches of brown colouring, is from the other side, apparently from somewhere above Rice Farm. The finished sketch shows the top of the tower of St. Just but the rest is concealed by houses. It gives the impression that a corner of the tower has fallen but this may only be an inaccurate drawing of the turret which covers the outlet of the newel stairs to the roof and naturally rises above the rest.

The unfinished sketch gives the impression that the tower is complete, but the roof is missing and the eastern gable rises well above the later roof inserted just below the level of the east window which can be seen above it.

In his visitation return of 1821, J. F. Howell, Vicar 1796- 1824, but non - resident, reported that there was a chapel in ruins in the Haven, but it was obviously still usable and continued to be used until shortly before the restoration in 1885.

Joseph Polsue, the compiler of Lake's Parochial History, recorded that the chapel had been partly repaired. This was doubtless done by David Jenkins, the Vicar 1824 - 1869, who, about 1862 bought out the Independents and instituted fortnightly weekday services, conducted by his curate. These were continued by C. R. Sowell (Vicar 1869 - 1903) who also taught the children there until "at last it became unsafe. The roof was beyond repair, the eastern gable was hanging inwards, the old windows were blocked up, the glass in the skylights was getting shattered, and the stairs were giving way, as a hint that it would be better not to use them. All this while the sky was visible through the roof of the tower". Under these circumstances, as rats clear out of a sinking ship, the Vicar took his class and congregation to the disused coast guard watch house on the beach. The restoration of the Parish Church having been completed... he undertook the restoration of St. Just at a cost of nearly £600.

THE RESTORATION AND AFTER

The restoration of 1885 was done by Piers St. Aubyn who ruined half the churches in Cornwall by his efficient but quite ruthless restorations, destroying countless ancient features of interest. Here, however he was surprisingly conservative. He must have overplastered the walls as he did at St. Goran where the plaster rises above the level of the cut stone of the arches. Subsequently an even worse mistake was made when the plaster was stripped. A generation ago there was an unhappy craze for this stripping of churches, but it is condemned by all authorities today. Every mediaeval church or chapel (unless built with smoothly finished cut stone on which murals could be painted direct) had the walls levelled up with a more or less thin coat of plaster to provide a surface for the mural paintings which were the ' visual aids' of those days when there were no books except costly manuscripts, very few could read, and many of the clergy were too ignorant to preach.

After restoration, the chapel was licensed by Bishop Wilkinson 27th May 1885 for the performance of Divine Service, for a school for religious services by a lay assistant and for meetings in connection with pastoral work. Also for baptisms but not for marriages or banns. One wedding has , however, been conducted here in recent years under special licence from the Archbishop of Canterbury.

DESCRIPTION OF THE CHURCH

The following description of the church is slightly abbreviated from Mr. M. H. N. Cuthbert Atchley's account in the booklet, now out of print, on the Parish of St. Goran compiled by Canon Doble from Henderson's notes.

"This chapel of ease...consists of a Chancel, Nave, and West Tower, although it is probable that parts of it rest on very ancient footings, the present Church is mainly of the late 15th century.

The windows are largely original and have beautiful interior Arches, which are an unusual feature in Cornwall. The lofty Tower Arch is a good example of Cornish work of its day. At the South end of the Altar is a late 15th, or early 16th century, granite bracket, apparently not in its original position, while to the North are two openings in the wall which may have formed the space for a holy well, the water of which seems to have flowed into this from outside the building.(cf. St. Clether's Holy Well Chapel). The visitor should notice the Altar Rails, made from purlins of a Cornish roof. They are the same as the remains of the roofs in the Parish Church and the Vicarage. Probably one covered the Church and the other the Chapel - of - ease. The present roof follows the lines of the old one which it has replaced.

Outside, the fine door of the Tower should be noted and specially the beautiful South Doorway and the niche over it, which once would have contained a figure of St. Just himself. The head of the niche is of a design that is rare except in Cornwall and the sister land of Brittany..."

The tower is very unusual. The newel staircase is not contained in a semi - detached turret but is accommodated within an extra angle, making the tower pentagonal. There are no less than five stone doorways leading from it - the entrance at the bottom, one into the gallery (originally perhaps a Squire's pew for Sir Henry Bodrugan), a third into a ringing chamber, a fourth into that containing the small bell, and a fifth leading onto the roof. In spite of the fine South doorway, the West door was clearly the one mainly used years ago as there is a fine Holy Water stoup just inside the tower arch.

Vestries or Sacristies were relatively uncommon in mediaeval days, and certainly the cramped space below the tower, now used as vestry, organ and ringing chamber combined could not have been so used when it was the main entrance into the chapel. The priest would have vested at the altar, vestments being kept in a chest underneath.

From the various references given to the state of the chapel from the 16th to the 19th centuries it is clear that even before the later restoration there must have been much rebuilding, particularly by Vicar Dalby about a hundred years before this. Unfortunately there is no record of what was done.- even in 1885. It is impossible to detect any junction of new and old masonry either within or without and it seems that the walls have been entirely re - faced inside and out. In the lower parts the core may be ancient, in the upper parts it is probably all modern. Thus the great problem of the church - the two recesses in the east wall and their relationship to one another - is likely to remain insoluble since it is impossible to say whether or not they have been tampered with in the course of ' restoration '.

Atchley's suggestions regarding the lower recess is probably correct and it is worth noting that the jambs and lintel are more crudely worked than the surround of the upper recess and maybe earlier in date. Moreover the left jamb seems to have been re - used as on the inside there is a groove across its width and a slot above the groove. It is possible that it is a relic of the earlier chapel left in place or re-used when Bodrugan rebuilt it.

*The St. Clether chapel (about 8 miles west of Launceston on the Camelford road) referred to by Atchley is of the greatest interest. It was restored but, unlike most ruins, had never been used as a quarry and had just crumbled and fallen untouched and therefore, except for a few minor details, the reconstruction can be relied upon for accuracy. Water from the Holy Well flowed through a covered granite channel into and through the north wall of the chapel, continuing through the east wall behind the altar and finally falling into a basin resembling a second holy well on the exterior but constructed within the thickness of the south wall. In the East wall in a position exactly corresponding to that of the lower recess at St. Just is a similar one believed to have been used for clearing leaves and twigs from the channel through the north wall.

Behind the south end of the altar is a second, differently shaped, recess (with rebate for a door) which is believed to have been an aumbry in which were placed relics of the saint. Water from the well flowed over the bones thereby acquiring still greater sanctity and could be drunk by those seeking cures from the exterior basin adjoining which is an opening (with hinge marks for a shutter) through which the priest could collect their offerings. Baring - Gould refers to a story in the Life of St. Patrick of a sacred well in which were soaked the bones of a Druid, the water then being drunk for healing: also a modern Welsh instance of patients drinking holy water from a part of the skull of St. Teilo.

There is no trace today of anything corresponding to these last features at St. Just (unless the frame of the upper recess could possibly be the re-used frame of one on the south side of the altar corresponding to that of St. Clether. It is the same shape). But a channel does run through the north wall from the lower recess to within about 3in. of the exterior, though excavation has failed to reveal any trace of a channel on the outside. The ground however has been disturbed and a little way out there are remains of a cobbled paving 10in. below the surface.

Above the top of the lower recess (4ft 10ins. from the present sanctuary floor) is a second recess with rebated stone frame. The interior is roughly circular and there are traces round the base of a clay lining, implying its use as an oven. So - called "Sacrament Ovens" are very rare, but about 20 have been recorded, some no longer extant and some very doubtful. But the wafers for the Communion were made by heating a runny paste of flour and water in a waffling iron over a glowing fire. "Sacrament Oven" is therefore a misnomer and they were probably used for baking the Holy Bread which was blessed, but not consecrated, and distributed each Sunday as a kind of substitute in days when very few indeed communicated more than once a year at Easter.

There can be little doubt that the upper recess was an oven, but it is difficult to imagine why it should have been placed at such a height. The present sanctuary floor is above the original floor level and steps would have been needed to reach the oven. Unless the whole thing has been inaccurately reconstructed at some restoration (which is exceedingly unlikely) it seems that the only motive must have been to prevent profanation by unauthorised use.